A Gift For

_____

From

_____

YOU WHO ANSWER

prayer,

TO YOU ALL PEOPLE

WILL COME.

PSALM 65:2

Prayer

Quiet Moments of
Intimacy with God

Our Daily Bread
Publishing™

Discovery House Publishers is affiliated with RBC Ministries,
Grand Rapids, Michigan.

Requests for permission to quote from this book should be
directed to: Permissions Department, Our Daily Bread Publishing,
PO Box 3566, Grand Rapids, MI 49501; or contact us by email at
permissionsdept@odb.org.

Scripture quotations taken from the Holy Bible, New International
Version Anglicised Copyright © 1979, 1984, 2011 Biblica. Used
by permission of Hodder & Stoughton Ltd, an Hachette UK
company. All rights reserved. 'NIV' is a registered trademark of
Biblica UK trademark number 1448790.

ISBN: 978-1-916718-31-9

Printed in the United Kingdom.

Introduction

You who answer prayer, to you all people will come.

PSALM 65:2

Prayer is a precious gift. Wherever we find ourselves, whatever we are facing, no matter how we are feeling and regardless of our circumstances, God invites us to draw near to His throne of grace in confidence. He hears and cares about our every prayer, even before they have left our hearts.

The writers of *Our Daily Bread* are here to walk alongside you as your companions throughout the triumphs and tragedies of life. Come as you are—raw, battered and beaten, unsure, questioning, dreaming or despairing—and they will open God's Word with you to help you draw close to the One who is only ever a prayer away.

We pray this book will help you draw near to Him. For He is right here, today and always.

In Him
Your Friends at Our Daily Bread Ministries

God's Timing

1 But God remembered Noah and all the wild animals and the livestock that were with him in the ark, and he sent a wind over the earth, and the waters receded. 2 Now the springs of the deep and the floodgates of the heavens had been closed, and the rain had stopped falling from the sky. 3 The water receded steadily from the earth. At the end of the hundred and fifty days the water had gone down, 4 and on the seventeenth day of the seventh month the ark came to rest on the mountains of Ararat. 5 The waters continued to recede until the tenth month, and on the first day of the tenth month the tops of the mountains became visible.

13 By the first day of the first month of Noah's six hundred and first year, the water had dried up from the earth. Noah then removed the covering from the ark and saw that the surface of the ground was dry. 14 By the twenty-seventh day of the second month the earth was completely dry.

15 Then God said to Noah, 16 'Come out of the ark, you and your wife and your sons and their wives. 17 Bring out every kind of living creature that is with you—the birds, the animals, and all the creatures that move along the ground—so they can multiply on the earth and be fruitful and increase in number on it.'

18 So Noah came out, together with his sons and his wife and his sons' wives.

—Genesis 8:1-5, 13-18

Mag had been looking forward to her planned trip to another country. But, as was her usual practice, she prayed about it first. "It's just a holiday," a friend remarked. "Why do you need to consult God?" Mag, however, believed in committing everything to Him. This time, she felt Him prompting her to cancel the trip. She did, and later—when she would have been there—an epidemic broke out in the country. "I feel like God was protecting me," she notes.

Noah too relied on God's protection as he and his family waited in the ark for nearly two months after the flood subsided. After being cooped up for more than ten months, he must have been eager to get out. After all, "the water had dried up from the earth" and "the ground was dry" (Genesis 8:13). But Noah didn't just rely on what he saw; instead, he left the ark only when God told him to (vv.15-19). He trusted that God had good reason for the extended wait—perhaps the ground wasn't completely safe yet.

As we pray about the decisions in our life, using our God-given faculties and waiting for His leading, we can trust in His timing, knowing that our wise Creator knows what is best for us. As the psalmist declared, "I trust in you, LORD . . . My times are in your hands" (Psalm 31:14-15).   —LESLIE KOH

Powerful Prayers

³⁶ At the time of sacrifice, the prophet Elijah stepped forward and prayed: 'Lord, the God of Abraham, Isaac and Israel, let it be known today that you are God in Israel and that I am your servant and have done all these things at your command. ³⁷ Answer me, Lord, answer me, so these people will know that you, Lord, are God, and that you are turning their hearts back again.'

³⁸ Then the fire of the Lord fell and burned up the sacrifice, the wood, the stones and the soil, and also licked up the water in the trench. ³⁹ When all the people saw this, they fell prostrate and cried, 'The Lord—he is God! The Lord—he is God!' ⁴⁰ Then Elijah commanded them, 'Seize the prophets of Baal. Don't let anyone get away!' They seized them, and Elijah had them brought down to the Kishon Valley and slaughtered there.

⁴¹ And Elijah said to Ahab, 'Go, eat and drink, for there is the sound of a heavy rain.' ⁴² So Ahab went off to eat and drink, but Elijah climbed to the top of Carmel, bent down to the ground and put his face between his knees.

⁴³ 'Go and look toward the sea,' he told his servant. And he went up and looked. 'There is nothing there,' he said. Seven times Elijah said, 'Go back.' ⁴⁴ The seventh time the servant reported, 'A cloud as small as a man's hand is rising from the sea.' So Elijah said, 'Go and tell Ahab, "Hitch up your chariot and go down before the rain stops you."' ⁴⁵ Meanwhile, the sky grew black with clouds, the wind rose, a heavy rainstorm came on and Ahab rode off to Jezreel.

—1 Kings 18:36–45

The gold medal was nearly his. Home favourite Matthew Hudson-Smith hurtled towards the finish line. Yet then, out of nowhere, a blur zoomed past. Zambian sprinter Muzala Samukonga suddenly found a furious burst of speed—from well behind the race leader—to snatch victory in Birmingham's 2022 Commonwealth 400m sprint.

The crowd's amazement quickly turned to shock and concern, however. Samukonga collapsed, vomiting and shaking violently. Dangerously exhausted, he was wheeled away for medical care.

The prophet Elijah knew that feeling too. He had just claimed a huge victory against false prophets who were leading Israel astray. "LORD, answer me, so these people will know that you, LORD, are God," he prayed (1 Kings 18:37), and fire rained down from heaven.

But then, as he asked God to end the severe drought, he couldn't have looked less like a champion. He "bent down to the ground and put his face between his knees" (v. 42). Wearied and weak, Elijah huddled up like a small child. Yet Scripture describes this prayer as "powerful and effective" (See James 5:16–18).

Have you ever felt like Elijah, trying to pray when life's race has drained you? Powerful prayers rise when we're weakest. For powerful prayers are not prayed by powerful people, but by weak people to their all-powerful God. In weakness, we entrust our needs to the One who can rain both fire and water from the sky (vv. 38, 45). God never lacks power.　　—CHRIS WALE

Prayer Matters

¹ In those days Hezekiah became ill and was at the point of death. The prophet Isaiah son of Amoz went to him and said, 'This is what the LORD says: put your house in order, because you are going to die; you will not recover.'

² Hezekiah turned his face to the wall and prayed to the LORD, ³ 'Remember, LORD, how I have walked before you faithfully and with wholehearted devotion and have done what is good in your eyes.' And Hezekiah wept bitterly.

⁴ Before Isaiah had left the middle court, the word of the LORD came to him: ⁵ 'Go back and tell Hezekiah, the ruler of my people, "This is what the LORD, the God of your father David, says: I have heard your prayer and seen your tears; I will heal you. On the third day from now you will go up to the temple of the LORD. ⁶ I will add fifteen years to your life. And I will deliver you and this city from the hand of the king of Assyria. I will defend this city for my sake and for the sake of my servant David."'

—2 KINGS 20:1-6

"Prayers for an upcoming brain scan." "That my kids would come back to church." "Comfort for Dave, who lost his wife." Our pastoral care team receives a weekly list of prayer requests like these so we can pray and send each person a hand-written note. The requests are overwhelming, and our efforts can feel small and unnoticed. That changed after I received a heartfelt thank-you card from Dave, the recently bereaved husband, with a copy of his beloved wife's obituary. I realised anew that prayer matters.

Jesus modelled that we should pray earnestly, often, and with hopeful faith. His time on earth was limited, but He prioritised getting away by Himself to pray (Mark 1:35; 6:46; 14:32).

Hundreds of years earlier, the Israelite king Hezekiah learned this lesson too. He was told that an illness would soon take his life (2 Kings 20:1). In distress and weeping bitterly, Hezekiah "turned his face to the wall and prayed to the LORD" (v. 2). In this instance, God's response was immediate. He healed Hezekiah's sickness, added fifteen years to his life, and promised to rescue the kingdom from an adversary (vv. 5-6). God answered his prayer not because Hezekiah was living a good life, but "for [his] own honour and for the sake of [his] servant David" (v. 6 NLT). We may not always receive what we ask for, but we can be sure that God is working in and through every prayer.

—KAREN PIMPO

Operating with Prayer

¹ After this, the Moabites and Ammonites with some of the Meunites came to wage war against Jehoshaphat.

² Some people came and told Jehoshaphat, 'A vast army is coming against you from Edom, from the other side of the Dead Sea. It is already in Hazezon Tamar' (that is, En Gedi). ³ Alarmed, Jehoshaphat resolved to enquire of the LORD, and he proclaimed a fast for all Judah. ⁴ The people of Judah came together to seek help from the Lord; indeed, they came from every town in Judah to seek him.

⁵ Then Jehoshaphat stood up in the assembly of Judah and Jerusalem at the temple of the LORD in the front of the new courtyard ⁶ and said:

'LORD, the God of our ancestors, are you not the God who is in heaven? You rule over all the kingdoms of the nations. Power and might are in your hand, and no one can withstand you. ⁷ Our God, did you not drive out the inhabitants of this land before your people Israel and give it for ever to the descendants of Abraham your friend? ⁸ They have lived in it and have built in it a sanctuary for your Name, saying, ⁹ "If calamity comes upon us, whether the sword of judgment, or plague or famine, we will stand in your presence before this temple that bears your Name and will cry out to you in our distress, and you will hear us and save us."

¹⁰ 'But now here are men from Ammon, Moab and Mount Seir, whose territory you would not allow Israel to invade when they came from Egypt; so they turned away from them and did not destroy them. ¹¹ See how they are repaying us by coming to drive us out of the possession you gave us as an inheritance. ¹² Our God, will you not judge them? For we have no power to face this vast army that is attacking us. We do not know what to do, but our eyes are on you.' —2 CHRONICLES 20:1–12

When my son needed orthopedic surgery, I was grateful for the doctor who performed the operation. The doctor, who was nearing retirement, assured us he'd helped thousands of people with the same problem. Even so, before the procedure, he prayed and asked God to provide a good outcome. And I'm so grateful He did.

Jehoshaphat, an experienced national leader, prayed too during a crisis. Three nations had united against him, and they were coming to attack his people. Although he had more than two decades of experience, he decided to ask God what to do. He prayed, "[We] will cry out to you in our distress, and you will hear us and save us" (2 Chronicles 20:9). He also asked for guidance, saying, "We do not know what to do, but our eyes are on you" (v. 12).

Jehoshaphat's humble approach to the challenge opened his heart to God's involvement, which came in the form of encouragement and divine intervention (vv. 15–17, 22). No matter how much experience we have in certain areas, praying for help develops a holy reliance on God. It reminds us that He knows more than we do, and He's ultimately in control. It puts us in a humble place—a place where He's pleased to respond and support us, no matter what the outcome may be.

—Jennifer Benson Schuldt

⁶ *So we rebuilt the wall till all of it reached half its height, for the people worked with all their heart.*

⁷ *But when Sanballat, Tobiah, the Arabs, the Ammonites and the people of Ashdod heard that the repairs to Jerusalem's walls had gone ahead and that the gaps were being closed, they were very angry.* ⁸ *They all plotted together to come and fight against Jerusalem and stir up trouble against it.* ⁹ *But we prayed to our God and posted a guard day and night to meet this threat.*

—Nehemiah 4:6–9

When Wallace and Mary Brown moved to an impoverished part of Birmingham, England, to pastor a dying church, they didn't know that a gang had made the grounds of their church and home its headquarters. The Browns had bricks thrown through their windows, their fences set on fire, and their children threatened. The abuse continued for months; the police were unable to stop it.

The book of Nehemiah recounts how the Israelites rebuilt Jerusalem's broken walls. When locals set out to "stir up trouble," threatening them with violence (Nehemiah 4:8), the Israelites "prayed to . . . God and posted a guard" (v. 9). Feeling God used this passage to direct them, the Browns, their children and a few others walked round their church's walls, praying that He would install angels as guards to protect them. The gang jeered, but the next day, only half of them showed up. The day after that, only five were there, and the day after, no one came. The Browns later heard the gang had given up terrorising people.

This miraculous answer to prayer isn't a formula for our own protection, but it's a reminder that opposition to God's work will come and must be fought with the weapon of prayer. "Remember the Lord, who is great and awesome," Nehemiah told the Israelites (v. 14). He can even set violent hearts free.

—Sheridan Voysey

Sweet Sleep

¹ LORD, how many are my foes!
   How many rise up against me!
² Many are saying of me,
   'God will not deliver him.'

³ But you, LORD, are a shield around me,
   my glory, the One who lifts my head high.
⁴ I call out to the LORD,
   and he answers me from his holy mountain.

⁵ I lie down and sleep;
   I wake again, because the LORD sustains me.
⁶ I will not fear though tens of thousands
   assail me on every side.

⁷ Arise, LORD!
   Deliver me, my God!
Strike all my enemies on the jaw;
   break the teeth of the wicked.

⁸ From the LORD comes deliverance.
   May your blessing be on your people.

—PSALM 3

Bad memories and accusing messages flooded Sal's mind. Sleep eluded him as fear filled his heart and sweat covered his skin. It was the night before his baptism, and he couldn't stop the onslaught of dark thoughts. Sal had received salvation in Jesus and knew that his sins had been forgiven, but the spiritual battle continued. It's then that his wife took his hand and prayed for him. Moments later, peace replaced the fear in Sal's heart. He got up and wrote the words he would share prior to being baptised—something he hadn't been able to do. After that, he experienced sweet sleep.

King David also knew what a restless night felt like. Fleeing from his son Absalom who wanted to steal his throne (2 Samuel 15–17), he knew that "tens of thousands [assailed him] on every side" (Psalm 3:6). David moaned, "How many are my foes!" (v. 1). Though fear and doubt could have won out, he called out to God, his "shield" (v. 3). Later, he found that he could "lie down and sleep . . . because the LORD sustains [him]" (v. 5).

When fears and struggles grip our mind and rest is replaced by restlessness, hope is found as we pray to God. While we might not experience immediate sweet sleep as Sal and David did, "in peace [we can] lie down and . . . dwell in safety" (4:8). For God is with us and He'll be our rest.   —TOM FELTEN

The One Who Answers Prayer

¹ *Praise awaits you, our God, in Zion;*
   to you our vows will be fulfilled.
² *You who answer prayer,*
   to you all people will come.
³ *When we were overwhelmed by sins,*
   you forgave our transgressions.
⁴ *Blessed are those you choose*
   and bring near to live in your courts!
We are filled with the good things of your house,
   of your holy temple.

⁵ *You answer us with awesome and righteous deeds,*
   God our Saviour,
the hope of all the ends of the earth
   and of the farthest seas.

—Psalm 65:1-5

*E*mma was stressed. She was due to attend her Universal Credit application meeting and had heard stories about how unfriendly the advisors could be. Yet her family really needed the financial support. Although not a Christian, she allowed the team at my wife's community support group to pray for her.

A week later it was a different story. Emma shared with them how amazing and helpful the advisor had been. "I've never heard of anyone having a meeting like mine. There's something in this prayer thing: maybe it's sending good vibes."

Clearly, Emma isn't yet understanding or acknowledging God, but isn't it exciting to see Him at work both in answering prayer and in drawing her to Himself? As the Psalmist writes, "Praise awaits you, our God, in Zion; to you our vows will be fulfilled. You who answer prayer, to you all people will come" (Psalm 65:1-2). We sometimes forget that God loves to answer prayer, showing Himself in the details of our and others' lives. In this, He invites us to come close to Him.

Sometimes we can't see God at work. And those times are incredibly hard. Yet Scripture promises, "You answer us with awesome and righteous deeds, God our Saviour" (v. 5). He hasn't changed. So, bring your needs to Him today, and don't give up, for He is still "the hope of all the ends of the earth" (v. 5).

—CHRIS WALE

Burdens Removed

¹ Sing for joy to God our strength;
   shout aloud to the God of Jacob!
² Begin the music, strike the tambourine,
   play the melodious harp and lyre.

³ Sound the ram's horn at the New Moon,
   and when the moon is full, on the day of our Feast;
⁴ this is a decree for Israel,
   an ordinance of the God of Jacob.
⁵ When God went out against Egypt,
   he established it as a statute for Joseph.

I heard an unknown voice say:

⁶ 'I removed the burden from their shoulders;
   their hands were set free from the basket.
⁷ In your distress you called and I rescued you,
   I answered you out of a thundercloud;
   I tested you at the waters of Meribah.
⁸ Hear me, my people, and I will warn you –
   if you would only listen to me, Israel!
⁹ You shall have no foreign god among you;
   you shall not worship any god other than me.
¹⁰ I am the LORD your God,
   who brought you up out of Egypt.
Open wide your mouth and I will fill it. —PSALM 81:1–10

I heard about an exasperated vicar who on Sundays would find crumpled-up balls of paper, always in the same row, when tidying up the church. After a few weeks, he unfolded one and discovered a heartfelt prayer. Moved, he decided to ask the person who sat nearby if these prayers were hers. "Yes," she replied, "I write my prayers in church, and then leave them here with God instead of taking them home with me!"

From then on, the vicar tidied up her prayers with a different attitude, breathing his own prayers for this woman. He echoed the psalmists in trusting that God would hear her pleas and lift her burdens. In Psalm 81, for instance, Asaph calls God's people to worship at a festival, giving thanks because God relieves them of their afflictions: "I heard an unknown voice say: 'I removed the burden from their shoulders; their hands were set free…" (Psalm 81:5–6). God rescues those who call on Him in their distress (v. 7).

Although Asaph's statement about rescue refers to God taking people out of their harmful life of slavery in Egypt, God still saves us today. We can release our burdens not only week by week but moment by moment, through writing out our prayers and balling them up, or simply by giving them to the Lord through our hearts and minds. He will hear us and save us.

—AMY BOUCHER PYE

No Plan B

¹ I lift up my eyes to the mountains –
  where does my help come from?
² My help comes from the LORD,
  the Maker of heaven and earth.

³ He will not let your foot slip –
  he who watches over you will not slumber;
⁴ indeed, he who watches over Israel
  will neither slumber nor sleep.

⁵ The LORD watches over you –
  the LORD is your shade at your right hand;
⁶ the sun will not harm you by day,
  nor the moon by night.

⁷ The LORD will keep you from all harm –
  he will watch over your life;
⁸ the LORD will watch over your coming and going
  both now and for evermore.

—PSALM 121

George Müller founded the Ashley Down orphanage in Bristol in 1854 where he cared for over 10,000 orphans. How did he do this? Faith-filled prayer! Daily he committed every need into God's hands.

Years before he opened the orphanage, he said, "The home will only be established if God provides the means and suitable staff to run it. . . . I don't look to Bristol, nor even to England, but to the living God, whose is the gold and the silver."

His principle of prayer echoes the words of the psalmist, who asked, "Where does my help come from?" (Psalm 121:1). Perhaps you're also asking where you should look for answers, for comfort, for provision. Notice the psalmist gives only one solution: "My help comes from the LORD, the Maker of heaven and earth" (v. 2).

The psalmist and George Müller both lived by the same principle, namely that help and provision come from God alone—through whatever means He determines. Sometimes we're tempted to create back-up plans in case God doesn't come through for us. Instead, we can take the promise of this psalm to heart: "He will not let your foot slip—he who watches over you will not slumber" (v. 3). All provision comes from the Maker of heaven and earth. We will find we have all we need when we keep our hope in Him alone.   —CHRIS WALE

No Need Is too Trivial

¹³ *Shout for joy, you heavens;*
rejoice, you earth;
burst into song, you mountains!
*For the L*ORD *comforts his people*
and will have compassion on his afflicted ones.

¹⁴ *But Zion said, 'The L*ORD *has forsaken me,*
*the L*ORD *has forgotten me.'*

¹⁵ *'Can a mother forget the baby at her breast*
and have no compassion on the child she has borne?
Though she may forget,
I will not forget you!
¹⁶ *See, I have engraved you on the palms of my hands;*
your walls are ever before me.
¹⁷ *Your children hasten back,*
and those who laid you waste depart from you.
¹⁸ *Lift up your eyes and look around;*
all your children gather and come to you.
*As surely as I live,' declares the L*ORD*,*
'you will wear them all as ornaments;
you will put them on, like a bride.   —ISAIAH 49:13-18

Several mothers of small children were sharing encouraging answers to prayer. Yet one woman said she felt selfish about troubling God with her personal needs. "Compared with the huge global needs God faces," she explained, "my circumstances must seem trivial to Him."

Moments later, her little son pinched his fingers in a door and ran screaming to his mother. She didn't say, "How selfish of you to bother me with your throbbing fingers when I'm busy!" She showed him great compassion and tenderness.

As Psalm 103:13 reminds us, "As a father has compassion on his children, so the LORD has compassion on those who fear him." In Isaiah 49, God said that even though a mother may forget to have compassion on her child, the Lord never forgets His children (v. 15). God assured His people, "I have engraved you on the palms of my hands" (v. 16).

Such intimacy with God belongs to those who fear Him and who rely on Him rather than on themselves. As that child with throbbing fingers ran freely to his mother, so may we run to God with our daily problems.

Our compassionate God doesn't neglect others to respond to our concerns. He has limitless time and love for each of His children. No need is too trivial for Him. —JOANIE YODER

God Will Answer

¹⁰ This is what the LORD says: 'When seventy years are completed for Babylon, I will come to you and fulfil my good promise to bring you back to this place. ¹¹ For I know the plans I have for you,' declares the LORD, 'plans to prosper you and not to harm you, plans to give you hope and a future. ¹² Then you will call on me and come and pray to me, and I will listen to you. ¹³ You will seek me and find me when you seek me with all your heart. ¹⁴ I will be found by you,' declares the LORD, 'and will bring you back from captivity. I will gather you from all the nations and places where I have banished you,' declares the LORD, 'and will bring you back to the place from which I carried you into exile.'

—JEREMIAH 29:10-14

When Pastor Timothy wears his preacher collar while traveling, he often gets stopped by strangers. "Pray for me, please," people in the airport say when they see the clerical band atop his simple dark suit. On a recent flight, a woman knelt by his seat when she noticed him, pleading: "Are you a pastor? Would you pray for me?" And Pastor Timothy prayed.

A passage in Jeremiah sheds light on why we perceive that God hears and answers prayer: God cares! He assured His beloved but sinful, exiled people, " 'For I know the plans I have for you,' declares the LORD, 'plans to prosper you and not to harm you' " (Jeremiah 29:11). God anticipated a time when they would return to Him. "Then you will call on me and come and pray to me," He said, "and I will listen to you. You will seek me and find me when you seek me with all your heart" (vv. 12-13).

The prophet learned this and more about prayer while confined to prison. God assured him, "Call to me and I will answer you and tell you great and unsearchable things you do not know" (33:3).

Jesus also urges us to pray. "Your Father knows what you need before you ask him," He said (Matthew 6:8). So "ask," "seek," and "knock" in prayer (7:7). Every petition we make draws us closer to the one who answers. We don't have to be a stranger to God in prayer. He knows us and wants to hear from us. We can take our concerns to Him right now.

—PATRICIA RAYBON

The Prayer of Jesus

⁵ 'And when you pray, do not be like the hypocrites, for they love to pray standing in the synagogues and on the street corners to be seen by others. Truly I tell you, they have received their reward in full. ⁶ But when you pray, go into your room, close the door and pray to your Father, who is unseen. Then your Father, who sees what is done in secret, will reward you. ⁷ And when you pray, do not keep on babbling like pagans, for they think they will be heard because of their many words. ⁸ Do not be like them, for your Father knows what you need before you ask him.

⁹ 'This, then, is how you should pray:
"'Our Father in heaven,
hallowed be your name,
¹⁰ your kingdom come,
your will be done,
    on earth as it is in heaven.
¹¹ Give us today our daily bread.
¹² And forgive us our debts,
    as we also have forgiven our debtors.
¹³ And lead us not into temptation,
    but deliver us from the evil one."'

¹⁴ For if you forgive other people when they sin against you, your heavenly Father will also forgive you. ¹⁵ But if you do not forgive others their sins, your Father will not forgive your sins.'

—MATTHEW 6:5–15

I was intrigued to hear how much Kate loves swimming in the lakes and rivers in England—in December. "How long do you stay in the water?" I asked. She replied, "Until I'm done . . . a bit like praying, I guess."

Kate's succinct answer points to a deeper truth in the Christian life, that there's no formula for prayer. But we can use the prayer Jesus taught His friends as a model (Matthew 6:9). And, of course, we can pray each part of it as little or as much as we feel right, until "we're done."

Jesus enjoyed an intimate relationship with His Father, and He welcomes us to address Him directly too: "Our Father in heaven" (v. 9). In the first half of the prayer we worship God, honouring Him and asking for His will to be done and His rule and reign to flourish on the earth (vv. 9–10). In the second half, we place our requests before God as we ask for our daily needs, that God would forgive us as we forgive others, and that He'd save us from temptation and trials (vv. 11–13).

Praying this prayer of Jesus helps us to focus on God and to ask for His help in our lives and in the world. We can trust that our Father knows our needs (v. 8) and that He loves to receive our prayers.

—AMY BOUCHER PYE

First on the List

^{25} 'Therefore I tell you, do not worry about your life, what you will eat or drink; or about your body, what you will wear. Is not life more than food, and the body more than clothes? ^{26} Look at the birds of the air; they do not sow or reap or store away in barns, and yet your heavenly Father feeds them. Are you not much more valuable than they? ^{27} Can any one of you by worrying add a single hour to your life?

^{28} 'And why do you worry about clothes? See how the flowers of the field grow. They do not labour or spin. ^{29} Yet I tell you that not even Solomon in all his splendour was dressed like one of these. ^{30} If that is how God clothes the grass of the field, which is here today and tomorrow is thrown into the fire, will he not much more clothe you—you of little faith? ^{31} So do not worry, saying, "What shall we eat?" or "What shall we drink?" or "What shall we wear?" ^{32} For the pagans run after all these things, and your heavenly Father knows that you need them. ^{33} But seek first his kingdom and his righteousness, and all these things will be given to you as well. ^{34} Therefore do not worry about tomorrow, for tomorrow will worry about itself. Each day has enough trouble of its own.'

—Matthew 6:25–34

The morning commenced with efficiency and precision. I practically jumped out of bed, launching into the teeth of the day's deadlines. Get the kids to school. *Check.* Get to work. *Check.* I blasted full throttle into writing my "To Do" list, in which personal and professional tasks tumbled together in an avalanche-like litany:

" . . . 13. Edit article. 14. Clean office. 15. Strategic team planning. 16. Write tech blog. 17. Clean basement. 18. Pray."

By the time I got to number eighteen, I'd remembered that I needed God's help. But I'd got that far before it even *occurred* to me that I was going at it alone, trying to manufacture my own momentum.

Jesus knew. He knew our days would crash one into another, a sea of ceaseless urgency. So He instructs, "Seek first [God's] kingdom and his righteousness, and all these things will be given to you as well" (Matthew 6:33).

It's natural to hear Jesus' words as a *command.* And they are. But there's more here—*an invitation.* In Matthew 6, Jesus invites us to exchange the world's frantic anxiety (vv. 25–32) for a life of trust, day by day. God, by His grace, helps us all of our days—even when we get to number eighteen on our list before we remember to see life from His perspective.

—ADAM R. HOLZ

Partnership with God

^{35} By this time it was late in the day, so his disciples came to him. 'This is a remote place,' they said, 'and it's already very late. ^{36} Send the people away so that they can go to the surrounding countryside and villages and buy themselves something to eat.'

^{37} But he answered, 'You give them something to eat.'

They said to him, 'That would take more than half a year's wages! Are we to go and spend that much on bread and give it to them to eat?'

^{38} 'How many loaves do you have?' he asked. 'Go and see.'

When they found out, they said, 'Five—and two fish.'

^{39} Then Jesus told them to make all the people sit down in groups on the green grass. ^{40} So they sat down in groups of hundreds and fifties. ^{41} Taking the five loaves and the two fish and looking up to heaven, he gave thanks and broke the loaves. Then he gave them to his disciples to distribute to the people. He also divided the two fish among them all. ^{42} They all ate and were satisfied, ^{43} and the disciples picked up twelve basketfuls of broken pieces of bread and fish. ^{44} The number of the men who had eaten was five thousand.

—MARK 6:35-44

When my friend and her husband struggled to conceive, doctors recommended she have a medical procedure done. But my friend was hesitant. "Shouldn't prayer be enough to fix our problem?" she said. "Do I really need to do the procedure?" My friend was trying to work out what role human action has in seeing God work.

The story of Jesus feeding the crowd can help us here (Mark 6:35-44). We may know how the story ends—thousands of people are miraculously fed with just a little bread and some fish (v. 42). But notice who is to feed the crowd? The disciples (v. 37). And who provides the food? They do (v. 38). Who distributes the food and cleans up afterward? The disciples (vv. 39-43). "You give them something to eat," Jesus said (v. 37). Jesus did the miracle, but it happened as the disciples acted.

A good crop is a gift from God (Psalm 65:9-10), but a farmer must still work the land. Jesus promised Peter "a catch" of fish but the fisherman still had to cast his nets (Luke 5:4-6). God can tend the earth and do miracles without us but typically chooses to work in a divine-human partnership.

My friend went through with the procedure and later successfully conceived. While this is no formula for a miracle, it was a lesson for my friend and me. God often does His miraculous work through the methods He's placed in our hands.

—SHERIDAN VOYSEY

Love through Prayer

^{27} 'But to you who are listening I say: love your enemies, do good to those who hate you, ^{28} bless those who curse you, pray for those who ill-treat you. ^{29} If someone slaps you on one cheek, turn to them the other also. If someone takes your coat, do not withhold your shirt from them. ^{30} Give to everyone who asks you, and if anyone takes what belongs to you, do not demand it back. ^{31} Do to others as you would have them do to you.' —LUKE 6:27–31

*F*or years, John had been somewhat of an irritant at church. He was bad-tempered, demanding and often rude. He complained constantly about not being served well, and about volunteers and staff not doing their job. He was, honestly, hard to love.

So when I heard that he'd been diagnosed with cancer, I found it difficult to pray for him. Memories of his harsh words and unpleasant character filled my mind. But remembering Jesus' call to love, I was drawn to say a simple prayer for John each day. A few days later, I found myself beginning to think a bit less often about his unlikeable qualities. *He must be really hurting,* I thought. *Perhaps he's feeling really lost now.*

Prayer, I realised, opens ourselves, our feelings and our relationships with others to God, allowing Him to enter and bring His perspective into it all. The act of submitting our will and feelings to Him in prayer allows the Holy Spirit to change our hearts, slowly but surely. No wonder Jesus' call to love our enemies is bound up tightly with a call to prayer: "Pray for those who mistreat you" (Luke 6:28).

I have to admit, I still struggle to think well of John. But with the Spirit's help, I'm learning to see him through God's eyes and heart—as a person to be forgiven and loved.

—LESLIE KOH

Persist in Praying

¹ Then Jesus told his disciples a parable to show them that they should always pray and not give up. ² He said: 'In a certain town there was a judge who neither feared God nor cared what people thought. ³ And there was a widow in that town who kept coming to him with the plea, "Grant me justice against my adversary."

⁴ 'For some time he refused. But finally he said to himself, "Even though I don't fear God or care what people think, ⁵ yet because this widow keeps bothering me, I will see that she gets justice, so that she won't eventually come and attack me!"'

⁶ And the Lord said, 'Listen to what the unjust judge says. ⁷ And will not God bring about justice for his chosen ones, who cry out to him day and night? Will he keep putting them off? ⁸ I tell you, he will see that they get justice, and quickly. However, when the Son of Man comes, will he find faith on the earth?'

—LUKE 18:1-8

Mila, a baking assistant, felt too helpless to defend herself when her supervisor accused her of pilfering some raisin bread. The unfounded assertion and corresponding salary deduction were just two of many wrongful actions from her supervisor. "God, please help," Mila prayed each day. "It's so hard working under her, but I need this job."

Jesus tells of a widow who also felt helpless and "sought justice against [her] adversary" (Luke 18:3). She turned to someone with the authority to resolve her case—a judge. Despite knowing that the judge was unjust, she persisted in approaching him.

The judge's eventual response (vv. 4-5) is infinitely different from that of our heavenly Father, who quickly responds with love and help (v. 7). If persistence could cause an unjust judge to take up a widow's case, how much more can and will God, who is the just Judge, do for us (vv. 7-8)? We can trust Him "to bring about justice for his chosen ones" (v. 7) and being persistent in praying is one way of showing our trust. We persist because we have faith that God will respond in perfect wisdom to our situation.

Eventually, Mila's supervisor resigned after other employees complained about her behaviour. As we walk in obedience to God, let's persist in praying, knowing the power of our prayers lies in the One who hears and helps us.   —KAREN HUANG

A Prayer for God's Will

41 He withdrew about a stone's throw beyond them, knelt down and prayed, 42 'Father, if you are willing, take this cup from me; yet not my will, but yours be done.' 43 An angel from heaven appeared to him and strengthened him. 44 And being in anguish, he prayed more earnestly, and his sweat was like drops of blood falling to the ground.

—LUKE 22:41-44

As a young believer in Jesus, I picked up my new devotional Bible and read a familiar Scripture: "Ask and it will be given to you" (Matthew 7:7). The commentary explained that what we really should be asking God for is our will to line up with His. By seeking for His will to be done, we would be assured that we'd receive what we asked for. That was a new concept for me, and I prayed for God's will to be done in my life.

Later that same day, I became surprisingly excited about a job opportunity I'd already turned down in my mind, and I was reminded about my prayer. Perhaps what I didn't think I wanted was actually a part of God's will for my life. I continued to pray and eventually accepted the job.

In a much more profound and eternally significant moment, Jesus modelled this for us. Before His betrayal and arrest, which led to His crucifixion, He prayed: "Father, if you are willing, take this cup from me; yet not my will, but yours be done" (Luke 22:42). Christ's prayer was filled with anguish and agony as He faced physical and emotional pain (v. 44). Yet He was still able to "earnestly" pray for God's will to be done.

God's will in my life has become my ultimate prayer. This means I may desire things I don't even know I want or need. The job I originally hadn't wanted turned out to be the beginning of my journey in Christian publishing. Looking back, I believe God's will was done.

—KATARA PATTON

Loving Our Enemy

⁶³ The men who were guarding Jesus began mocking and beating him. ⁶⁴ They blindfolded him and demanded, 'Prophesy! Who hit you?' ⁶⁵ And they said many other insulting things to him.

³² Two other men, both criminals, were also led out with him to be executed. ³³ When they came to the place called the Skull, they crucified him there, along with the criminals—one on his right, the other on his left. ³⁴ Jesus said, 'Father, forgive them, for they do not know what they are doing.' And they divided up his clothes by casting lots.

³⁵ The people stood watching, and the rulers even sneered at him. They said, 'He saved others; let him save himself if he is God's Messiah, the Chosen One.'

³⁶ The soldiers also came up and mocked him. They offered him wine vinegar ³⁷ and said, 'If you are the king of the Jews, save yourself.'

³⁸ There was a written notice above him, which read: THIS IS THE KING OF THE JEWS.

—Luke 22:63-65; 23:32-38

*D*uring World War II, medic Lynne Weston went ashore with the marines as they stormed enemy-held islands. Inevitably, there were gruesome casualties. He did his best to patch up wounded combatants for evacuation. On one occasion, his unit encountered an enemy soldier with a bad abdominal wound. Due to the nature of the injury, the man couldn't be given water. To keep him alive, Petty Officer Weston administered intravenous plasma.

"Save that plasma for *our* fellas!" bellowed one of the marines. Weston ignored him. He knew what Jesus would do: "love your enemies" (Matthew 5:44).

Jesus did far more than speak those challenging words; He lived them. When a hostile mob seized Him and took Him to the high priest, "the men who were guarding Jesus began mocking and beating him" (Luke 22:63). The abuse continued all the way through His sham trials and execution. Jesus didn't merely endure it. When Roman soldiers crucified Him, *He prayed for their forgiveness* (23:34).

We may not encounter a literal enemy who's trying to kill us. But everyone knows what it's like to endure ridicule and scorn. Our natural reaction is to respond in anger. Jesus raised the bar: "pray for those who persecute you" (Matthew 5:44).

Today, let's walk in *that* kind of love, showing kindness as Jesus did—even to our enemies. —TIM GUSTAFSON

Seven Minutes of Terror

³⁸ *Jesus, once more deeply moved, came to the tomb. It was a cave with a stone laid across the entrance.* ³⁹ *'Take away the stone,' he said.*

'But, Lord,' said Martha, the sister of the dead man, 'by this time there is a bad odour, for he has been there four days.'

⁴⁰ *Then Jesus said, 'Did I not tell you that if you believe, you will see the glory of God?'*

⁴¹ *So they took away the stone. Then Jesus looked up and said, 'Father, I thank you that you have heard me.* ⁴² *I knew that you always hear me, but I said this for the benefit of the people standing here, that they may believe that you sent me.'*

⁴³ *When he had said this, Jesus called in a loud voice, 'Lazarus, come out!'*

—John 11:38–43

When the Mars rover *Perseverance* landed on that red planet on 18 February, 2021, those monitoring its arrival endured "seven minutes of terror". As the spacecraft ended its 292-million-mile journey, it went through a complex landing procedure it had to do on its own. Signals from Mars to Earth take several minutes, so NASA couldn't hear from *Perseverance* during the landing. Not being in contact was frightening for the team who had put so much effort and resources into the mission.

Sometimes we may experience our own times of fear when we feel we're not hearing from God—we pray but we don't get answers. In Scripture, we find people getting answers to prayer quickly (see Daniel 9:20–23) and those not getting answers for a long time (see Hannah's story in 1 Samuel 1:10–20). Perhaps the most poignant example of a delayed answer—one that surely struck terror in the hearts of Mary and Martha—was when they asked Jesus to help their sick brother Lazarus (John 11:3). Jesus delayed, and their brother died (vv. 6–7, 14–15). Yet four days later, Christ answered by resurrecting Lazarus (vv. 43–44).

Waiting for answers to our prayers can be difficult. But God can comfort and help as we "approach [His] throne of grace with confidence, . . . [that] we may receive mercy and find grace to help us in our time of need" (Hebrews 4:16).

—Dave Branon

The Speed of Joy

9 'As the Father has loved me, so have I loved you. Now remain in my love. 10 If you keep my commands, you will remain in my love, just as I have kept my Father's commands and remain in his love. 11 I have told you this so that my joy may be in you and that your joy may be complete.'

—JOHN 15:9-11

Go at the speed of joy. The phrase dropped into my mind as I prayerfully considered the year ahead one morning, and it seemed apt. I had a propensity to overwork, which often sapped my joy. So, following this guidance, I committed to working at an enjoyable pace in the coming year, making space for friends and joyful activities.

This plan worked . . . until March! Then I partnered with a university to oversee the trial of a course I'd been developing. With students to enrol and teaching to deliver, I was soon working long hours to keep up. How could I *go at the speed of joy* now?

Jesus promises joy to those who believe in Him, telling us it comes through remaining in His love (John 15:9) and prayerfully bringing our needs to Him (16:24). "I have told you this so that my *joy* may be in you and that your *joy* may be complete," he says (15:11). This joy comes as a gift through His Spirit, who we're to keep in step with (Galatians 5:22-25). I found I could only maintain joy during my busy period when I spent time each night in restful, trusting prayer.

Since joy is so important, it makes sense to prioritise it in our schedules. But since life is never completely under our control, I'm glad another source of joy—the Spirit—is available to us. For me, going at the speed of joy now means going at the speed of prayer—making time to receive from the Joy-Giver.

—SHERIDAN VOYSEY

Tongue-Tied in Prayer

22 We know that the whole creation has been groaning as in the pains of childbirth right up to the present time. 23 Not only so, but we ourselves, who have the firstfruits of the Spirit, groan inwardly as we wait eagerly for our adoption to sonship, the redemption of our bodies. 24 For in this hope we were saved. But hope that is seen is no hope at all. Who hopes for what they already have? 25 But if we hope for what we do not yet have, we wait for it patiently.

26 In the same way, the Spirit helps us in our weakness. We do not know what we ought to pray for, but the Spirit himself intercedes for us through wordless groans. 27 And he who searches our hearts knows the mind of the Spirit, because the Spirit intercedes for God's people in accordance with the will of God.

—ROMANS 8:22–27

When my baby brother underwent surgery, I was concerned. My mother explained that "tongue-tie" (*ankyloglossia*) was a condition he was born with and that without help, his ability to eat and eventually to speak would be hindered. Today we use the term tongue-tied to describe being at a loss for words or too shy to speak.

Sometimes we can be tongue-tied in prayer, not knowing what to say. Our tongues tie up in spiritual clichés and repetitive phrases. We arrow our emotions heavenward, wondering if they will reach God's ears. Our thoughts zigzag along an unfocused path.

Writing to first-century Roman believers in Christ, the apostle Paul addressed what to do when we struggle to know how to pray, inviting us to find help from the Holy Spirit. "The Spirit helps us in our weakness. We do not know what we ought to pray for, but the Spirit himself intercedes for us through wordless groans" (Romans 8:26). The concept of "help" here is to carry a heavy load. And "wordless groans" indicates an interceding presence as the Spirit carries our needs to God.

When we're tongue-tied in prayer, God's Spirit helps shape our confusion, pain and distraction into the perfect prayer that moves from our hearts to God's ears. He listens and answers, bringing the exact kind of comfort we may not have known we needed until we asked Him to pray for us.   —ELISA MORGAN

Pray Something Else

. . . .

[12] Therefore, I urge you, brothers and sisters, in view of God's mercy, to offer your bodies as a living sacrifice, holy and pleasing to God—this is your true and proper worship. [2] Do not conform to the pattern of this world, but be transformed by the renewing of your mind. Then you will be able to test and approve what God's will is—his good, pleasing and perfect will.

—ROMANS 12:1-2

. . . .

*H*aving taxied to the runway with a squirming toddler (who had to stay buckled in until airborne), my flight was suddenly delayed. Agonising minutes passed. The in-flight entertainment clicked on. "Oh no, please Lord, don't let it be an hour," I prayed. And when the next sitcom episode started, "Please Lord, not two hours."

"Pray something else!" I felt God say. So instead of praying for a change of circumstances, I asked for what I needed to endure them: "Lord, give me grace to look after my child for as long as this delay takes."

I learnt a valuable lesson that day about God's "good, pleasing and perfect will" (Romans 12:2). Sometimes, He isn't just going to 'airlift' me out of tough times; He wants me to seek His strength and presence through them. I think this is part of what Paul means when he calls us to be a "living sacrifice" (Romans 12:1). No longer am I living for my own agenda but surrendering to God's.

"Be transformed," Paul says (v. 2). Or, as God prompted me, "Pray something else." Rather than only asking God to change our adverse circumstances (a very natural response), God invites us to entrust our needs and circumstances to Him.

Of course, we can always pray for rescue. But perhaps we can learn to seek something deeper too: "Lord, show me Your will in this; give me what I need to endure it."

—DEBBI FRALICK

Don't lose Heart

16 Therefore we do not lose heart. Though outwardly we are wasting away, yet inwardly we are being renewed day by day. 17 For our light and momentary troubles are achieving for us an eternal glory that far outweighs them all. 18 So we fix our eyes not on what is seen, but on what is unseen, since what is seen is temporary, but what is unseen is eternal. —2 Corinthians 4:16–18

I don't remember a time when my mum Dorothy was in good health. For many years as a brittle diabetic, her blood sugar was wildly erratic. Complications developed and her damaged kidneys necessitated permanent dialysis. Neuropathy and broken bones resulted in the use of a wheelchair. Her eyesight began to regress towards blindness.

But as her body failed her, Mum's prayer life grew more vigorous. She spent hours praying for others to know and experience the love of God. Precious words of Scripture grew sweeter to her. Before her eyesight faded, she wrote a letter to her sister Marjorie including words from 2 Corinthians 4: "We do not lose heart. Though outwardly we are wasting away, yet inwardly we are being renewed day by day" (v. 16).

The apostle Paul knew how easy it is to "lose heart". In 2 Corinthians 11, he describes his life—one of danger, pain and deprivation (vv. 23–29). Yet he viewed those "troubles" as temporary. And he encouraged us to think not only about what we see but also about what we can't see—that which is *eternal* (4:17–18).

Despite what's happening to us, our loving Father is continuing our inner renewal every day. His presence with us is sure. Through the gift of prayer, He's only a breath away. And His promises to strengthen us and give us hope and joy remain true.

—CINDY HESS KASPER

Capturing Our Destructive Thoughts

2 I beg you that when I come I may not have to be as bold as I expect to be towards some people who think that we live by the standards of this world. 3 For though we live in the world, we do not wage war as the world does. 4 The weapons we fight with are not the weapons of the world. On the contrary, they have divine power to demolish strongholds. 5 We demolish arguments and every pretension that sets itself up against the knowledge of God, and we take captive every thought to make it obedient to Christ

—2 CORINTHIANS 10:2–5

*D*ebbie was just twelve when a man in his twenties groomed her. Like many girls who are sexually abused, she couldn't recognise the relationship as harmful and even defended her 'boyfriend'. Her Christian parents labelled her as a 'rebellious' teen, especially when she started taking drugs and self-harming. Desperate, her older sister Arianna got Debbie a place at a residential discipleship programme, Mercy Multiplied International. Seven months later Debbie returned with new life and hope.

Now Arianna and Debbie run Mercy UK, where they help other young women struggling with addiction or mental illness. It's not about focusing on behaviour but dealing with the core problem. Where, following abuse, the women have absorbed strong internal messages like "I'm a failure" or "I'm worth nothing", Arianna helps them replace that negative self-talk with biblical truths about how Jesus sees them. When they believe they are worthy of true love, transformation follows.

Arianna sees this as fulfilling Paul's instruction to "take captive every thought" (2 Corinthians 10:5). This includes false teaching: "We demolish arguments and every pretension that sets itself up against the knowledge of God" (v. 5), but also our own misplaced shame. Wonderfully, through prayer, we have spiritual "weapons" that have "divine power to demolish strongholds" (v. 4), so even lifelong destructive patterns can be changed. Today consider your own internal messages. What might God say over you instead? —Tanya Marlow

The Grace Exchange

⁶ Even if I should choose to boast, I would not be a fool, because I would be speaking the truth. But I refrain, so no one will think more of me than is warranted by what I do or say, ⁷ or because of these surpassingly great revelations. Therefore, in order to keep me from becoming conceited, I was given a thorn in my flesh, a messenger of Satan, to torment me. ⁸ Three times I pleaded with the Lord to take it away from me. ⁹ But he said to me, 'My grace is sufficient for you, for my power is made perfect in weakness.' Therefore I will boast all the more gladly about my weaknesses, so that Christ's power may rest on me. ¹⁰ That is why, for Christ's sake, I delight in weaknesses, in insults, in hardships, in persecutions, in difficulties. For when I am weak, then I am strong.

—2 Corinthians 12:6–10

In 1967, at only seventeen years old, Joni Eareckson broke her neck in a diving accident. Left quadriplegic from the shoulders down, she begged God to heal her. But it was not to be. God, however, had redemptive plans for His child following this human tragedy. Plans that, through Joni, would transform the lives of millions of people with disabilities and demonstrate God's love and grace to those who suffer in this broken world.

Centuries earlier God told Paul, tormented by an unnamed condition, that He would not answer his pleas for healing (2 Corinthians 12:8). Instead, the Lord explained to the suffering apostle, "my power is made perfect in weakness" (v. 9). Paul's ministry was not a way to accrue boasting rights (v. 7) but to fulfil God's plan. So, in His love for Paul and for the many waiting to hear the gospel, God promised something other than healing. He promised him grace—sufficient and enabling for all that God was asking—grace accompanied by *Christ's power* (v. 9). That delivered more than a healthy Paul ever could!

God is in the transformation business, but not always in the way we want. Consider, for instance, how He has used Joni as a living example of His grace and power. He trusts us to surrender the unexplained and, in exchange, to receive Christ's power. That's some trade!　　　　　　　　　—CATHERINE CAMPBELL

Pause to Pray

⁴ Rejoice in the Lord always. I will say it again: rejoice! ⁵ Let your gentleness be evident to all. The Lord is near. ⁶ Do not be anxious about anything, but in every situation, by prayer and petition, with thanksgiving, present your requests to God. ⁷ And the peace of God, which transcends all understanding, will guard your hearts and your minds in Christ Jesus.

⁸ Finally, brothers and sisters, whatever is true, whatever is noble, whatever is right, whatever is pure, whatever is lovely, whatever is admirable—if anything is excellent or praiseworthy—think about such things. ⁹ Whatever you have learned or received or heard from me, or seen in me—put it into practice. And the God of peace will be with you. —PHILIPPIANS 4:4-9

A meteorologist went viral for uttering six simple yet profound words during his weather forecast on 24 March, 2023. Matt Laubhan was tracking a severe storm when he realised a catastrophic tornado was about to bear down on one town in particular. That's when Laubhan paused on live TV to say this prayer heard worldwide: "Dear Jesus, please help them. Amen." Some viewers later said that prayer prompted them to take cover. His spontaneous and heartfelt prayer may have helped save countless lives.

Our prayers can make a difference too. They don't have to be long-winded. They can be short and sweet and can be said at any time of the day. Whether we're at work, running errands or on holiday, we can "pray continually" (1 Thessalonians 5:17).

God loves to hear us pray throughout the day. The apostle Paul reminds us that we don't have to be prisoners of worry or fear but can take all our cares and concerns to God: "Do not be anxious about anything, but in every situation, by prayer and petition, with thanksgiving, present your requests to God. And the peace of God, which transcends all understanding, will guard your hearts and your minds in Christ Jesus" (Philippians 4:6-7).

Whether we're enjoying a sunny day or being hit by the literal or figurative storms of life, let's remember to pause and pray throughout the day. —NANCY GAVILANES

The Watchmaker's Shop

¹⁵ *Let the peace of Christ rule in your hearts, since as members of one body you were called to peace. And be thankful.* ¹⁶ *Let the message of Christ dwell among you richly as you teach and admonish one another with all wisdom through psalms, hymns, and songs from the Spirit, singing to God with gratitude in your hearts.* ¹⁷ *And whatever you do, whether in word or deed, do it all in the name of the Lord Jesus, giving thanks to God the Father through him.*

—Colossians 3:15–17

The shop routine always started with a Bible reading, customers were welcomed with grace, and "if there were problems, we prayed over them together".

Working in her father's watchmaker's shop in the 1920s was foundational in Corrie Ten Boom's life. She learned patience as she repaired delicate time pieces, and how to depend upon the Lord for every task. "When my hand was not steady and I had to do a very exacting piece of work, . . . I prayed, 'Lord Jesus, will You lay Your hand on my hand?' He always did, and our joined hands worked securely. Jesus never fails us for a moment."

That watchmaker's shop was infused with the peace and joy of Christ's presence, not unlike Paul's teaching to the church in Colossae: "Let the message of Christ dwell among you richly. . . . And whatever you do, whether in word or deed, do it all in the name of the Lord Jesus" (Colossians 3:16–17). *Whatever* you do. From serving customers at work to supporting family at home, Jesus is in every action. We can always ask for His hands to steady and strengthen us.

In the watchmaker's shop, Corrie Ten Boom realised that "God's love and power are available to us in the trivial things of everyday life". What ordinary tasks lie ahead of you today? When we meet the Lord there, these can become uplifting moments of His grace and provision. —CHRIS WALE

Devoted to Prayer

2 Devote yourselves to prayer, being watchful and thankful. 3 And pray for us, too, that God may open a door for our message, so that we may proclaim the mystery of Christ, for which I am in chains. 4 Pray that I may proclaim it clearly, as I should. 5 Be wise in the way you act towards outsiders; make the most of every opportunity. 6 Let your conversation be always full of grace, seasoned with salt, so that you may know how to answer everyone.

12 Epaphras, who is one of you and a servant of Christ Jesus, sends greetings. He is always wrestling in prayer for you, that you may stand firm in all the will of God, mature and fully assured. 13 I vouch for him that he is working hard for you and for those at Laodicea and Hierapolis. —COLOSSIANS 4:2-6, 12-13

"I've been praying for you for fifty years," said the elderly woman. My friend Lou looked into her eyes with profound gratitude. He was visiting the Bulgarian village that his father grew up in and left as a teenager. The woman, a believer in Jesus, lived next to his grandparents. She began to pray for Lou as soon she heard about his birth a continent away. Now, over half a century later, he was visiting the village on a business trip, and while there he spoke to a group about his faith. Lou hadn't become a believer in Jesus until he was almost thirty, and when this woman approached him after he spoke, he wondered about the impact her persistent prayers had made on his journey to faith.

We'll never know the full effect of our prayers this side of heaven. But Scripture gives us this counsel: "Devote yourselves to prayer, being watchful and thankful" (Colossians 4:2). When Paul wrote those words to believers in the small city of Colossae, he also asked for prayer himself so that God would "open a door" for his message wherever he went (v. 3).

Sometimes we may think, *I don't have the spiritual gift of prayer.* But of all the spiritual gifts listed in the Bible, prayer isn't among them. Perhaps this is because God longs for each of us to pray faithfully, so that we may see what only He can do.

—JAMES BANKS

Pray Always

16 Rejoice always, 17 pray continually, 18 give thanks in all circumstances; for this is God's will for you in Christ Jesus.

19 Do not quench the Spirit. 20 Do not treat prophecies with contempt 21 but test them all; hold on to what is good, 22 reject every kind of evil. —1 THESSALONIANS 5:16-22

I got an 84 on the test!

I felt my teen's excitement as I read her message on my phone. She'd just started attending classes at a high school and was using her phone during lunch. My heart leaped, not just because my daughter had done well on a challenging test, but because she was choosing to communicate it to me. She wanted to share her good news with me!

Realising that her text had made my day, I later thought about how God must feel when I reach out to Him. Is He as pleased when I talk to Him? Prayer is how we communicate with God and something we're told to do "continually" (1 Thessalonians 5:17). Talking with Him reminds us that He's with us through the good and the bad. Sharing our news with God, even though He already knows all about us, is helpful as it shifts our focus and helps us think about Him. Isaiah 26:3 says, "You will keep in perfect peace those whose minds are steadfast [fixed on you], because they trust in you." We have peace awaiting us when we turn our attention to God.

Regardless of what we face, may we continually speak with God and keep in touch with our Creator and Saviour. Whisper a prayer and remember to rejoice and "give thanks." After all, Paul says, this is "God's will" for us (1 Thessalonians 5:18).

—KATARA PATTON

Remember in Prayer

. . . .

¹ *Paul, a prisoner of Christ Jesus, and Timothy our brother,*

To Philemon our dear friend and fellow worker—² also to Apphia our sister and Archippus our fellow soldier—and to the church that meets in your home:

³ *Grace and peace to you from God our Father and the Lord Jesus Christ.*

⁴ *I always thank my God as I remember you in my prayers.*

—PHILEMON 1:1–4

. . . .

Malcolm Cloutt was named a 2021 Maundy Money honouree by Queen Elizabeth II—an annual service award. Cloutt, who was one hundred years old at the time of the recognition, was honoured for having given out one thousand Bibles during his lifetime. Cloutt has kept a record of everyone who's received a Bible and has prayed for them regularly.

Cloutt's faithfulness in prayer is a powerful example of the kind of love we find throughout Paul's writings in the New Testament. Paul often assured the recipients of his letters that he was regularly praying for them. To his friend Philemon, he wrote, "I always thank my God as I remember you in my prayers" (Philemon 1:4). In his letter to Timothy, Paul wrote, "Night and day I constantly remember you in my prayers" (2 Timothy 1:3). To the church in Rome, Paul emphasised that he remembered them in prayer "constantly" and "at all times" (Romans 1:9–10).

While we might not have a thousand people to pray for like Malcolm, intentional prayer for those we know is powerful because God responds to our prayers. When prompted and empowered by His Spirit to pray for a specific individual, I've found a simple prayer calendar can be a useful tool. Dividing names into a daily or weekly calendar helps me be faithful to pray. What a beautiful demonstration of love when we remember others in prayer.
—Lisa M. Samra

6 Promises in Scripture about Your Prayers

1 You answer us with awesome and righteous deeds, God our Saviour, the hope of all the ends of the earth and of the furthest seas.

PSALM 65:5

2 When you pray, go into your room, close the door and pray to your Father, who is unseen. Then your Father, who sees what is done in secret, will reward you.

MATTHEW 6:6

3 Ask and it will be given to you; seek and you will find; knock and the door will be opened to you.

MATTHEW 7:7

4   Do not be anxious about anything, but in
    every situation, by prayer and petition,
    with thanksgiving, present your requests to
    God. And the peace of God, which
    transcends all understanding, will guard
    your hearts and your minds in Christ Jesus.
    PHILIPPIANS 4:6-7

5   The prayer of a righteous person is
    powerful and effective.
    JAMES 5:16

6   This is the confidence we have in
    approaching God: that if we ask
    anything according to his will, he hears
    us. And if we know that he hears us—
    whatever we ask—we know that we
    have what we asked of him.
    1 JOHN 5:14-15